| DATE | | | |
|---|---|---|---|
| | | | |
| | | | |
| | | | |
| | | | |
| | | | |
| | | | |
| | | | |
| | | | |
| | | | |
| | | | |
| | | | |
| | | | |

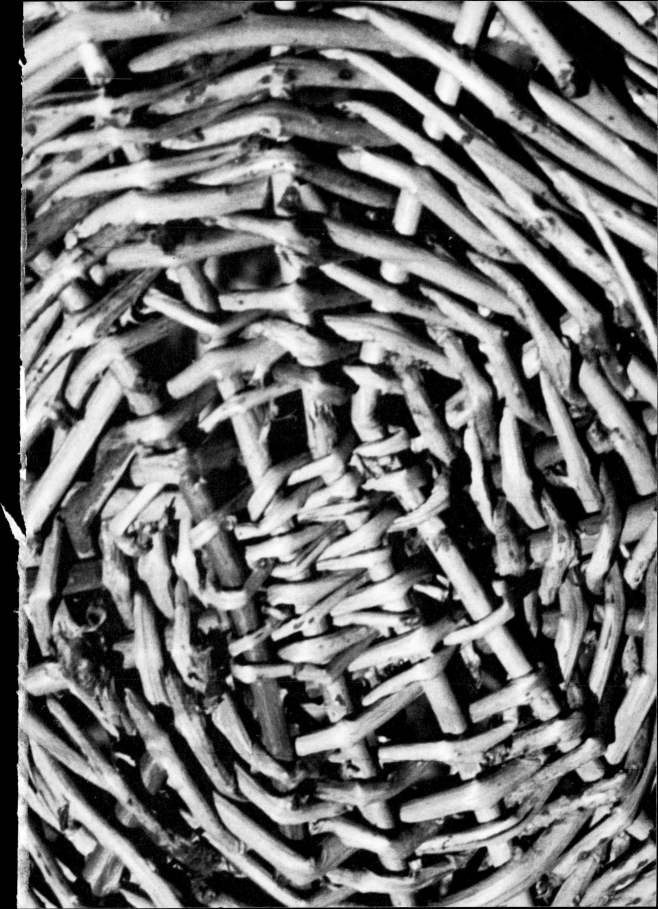

# MARA CARY

# BASIC BASKETS

## HOUGHTON MIFFLIN COMPANY

### BOSTON : 1975

The photographs in this book are by
Dick and Mara Cary.

Copyright © 1975 by Mara Cary

*Library of Congress Cataloging in Publication Data*

Cary, Mara.
  Basic baskets.

    1. Basket making.  I. Title.  II. Title:
Basic basket book.
TT879.B3C37     746.4'1     75–14222
ISBN 0–395–21626–5

Printed in the United States of America

A  10  9  8  7  6  5  4  3  2  1

*Dedicated to Bill and Andy, and we know why*

*thanks*

to my husband most of all
to Mitch and Carol
to Polly Bean
to Frank Conroy
to Betty Hogan
to Frances Tenenbaum
to Joyce White Van Voorst
to T. M.
to Granger Frost for his brambles
to all my students for teaching me so much
to David Voorhees for never believing me
and to Kathy-Kelm and Larry Cronin for believing always

# Contents

The pulse of times erases eons with a sigh,

And we, like gasps, pass quickly, night to night,

Allowed, by some grave joy, to have our breath.

Do not handle brightness lightly;

It is the deepest darkness of our candle flicker.

RICHARD MONTFORT CARY, 1965

# Introduction

The first time I made pickles, I had the help of several fine cookbooks, a set of canning jars with instructions, and a box of rubber rings with writing on the side, not to mention fresh green beans from my own garden. I mastered the recipe and sterilized the jars with little difficulty, but I couldn't get the rubber rings to stay in place. Well, it is a simple thing. One must stretch the ring a little, to fit over the rim, so that it rests on the lip provided for it. But no one had written down that instruction and as intelligent as we all claim to be, I couldn't figure it out.

Fortunately, I knew whom to call and finally my beans were safely sealed in their dill. There aren't many neighbors today who can tell you how to make baskets, so that is the purpose of this book.

Not quite five years ago, when our son was eighteen months old, my husband and I decided to seek soil in which to sink roots. In the four years of our marriage, we had moved thirteen times and somehow it seemed that if we stayed in one place we might be able to find some answers. Although it could be said we are part of the "back to earth" movement, we were not following any dictates save our own longings to be still.

We moved to Nantucket, promising ourselves that we would at least *say* we were going to stay for five years, which seemed forever at that time. Today we are only a few months shy of having reached our goal. The world is more confusing and outrageous than ever, but we have found some answers for ourselves in stillness. Our love has grown. After several more moves — even on Nantucket — we have built our own house and are doing our best to wrest a living out of the society of which we are a part. Slowly we are carving a new lifestyle. To some it might seem to be one that is looking backward, for it cherishes the homely, the rude, the unpackaged, the un-mechanized, the careful. We do not think of it as a blind shutting out of any visions of the future, but rather, for us, the right way to face the future. The carving is not easy. It is often painful. But in it are the seeds of sanity, of joy.

One problem I faced in Nantucket was what to do with myself. I had been used to working as an actress, looking for work and finding babysitters. Now I wanted to be my own babysitter for a few years. And while I have not abandoned acting, I have abandoned the job-hunting part of it. So I began trying some new things. Making pickles was not the only thing I learned to do. I began sewing. I learned to be a pretty good bread maker. I learned to garden, and never tire of the treat of eating our home-grown produce; each year our little plot ex-pands.

Above all, I learned to make baskets.

During our first summer on Nantucket, we felt ourselves extremely lucky to be allowed to live in an old barn. As on most island resorts, housing on Nantucket for people in our economic bracket is virtually impossible to come by. The old barn sat alone in the middle of an enormous rolling field. We roughed it, going to bed at dusk when the mosquitoes came out, because the only place to avoid them was under a canopy of netting. We walked the dusty road. It was beauti-ful.

It was in that barn one morning that a friend suggested to me that I try making baskets — and promptly presented me with some reed and a little booklet that "told how." (He had tried baskets but found he was more intrigued with carpentry.) So I found four old books in the library and taught myself. And I located a market for the baskets I made. Most important, though, was that I found in weaving baskets an activity that has come to have profound meaning for me. Most of the baskets I make take between two and eight hours to complete. Recently I made one that took about fifty hours of labor. Those fifty-odd hours were peaceful and the basket is beautiful to me. It will be useful for many years.

I had scarcely taught myself how to weave baskets when people around me asked me to show them how, too. So I did. And soon I organized classes. I worked very hard on explaining the processes, on communicating the technique, on being a good teacher. This book is a natural manifestation of that work.

The pamphlet I first learned from was explicit, but the baskets were not the kind I wanted to make. What I did want to do, and am doing now, has grown from a process of trial and retrial, of using a technique from one book with the material suggested by another, and so on. Growth is eclectic. And quite by chance I became aware of the basis from which all the techniques I use grew and I began teaching my "basic basket." The more I taught it, the more I understood why it was a good way for someone to get started. For example, an essential part of the "basic basket" is twining, a weave done with two weavers. Now, this is not as simple, intellectually, as a plain weave done with one weaver. But weaving a basket is not an intellectual process. It is a mechanical one, and thus the learning of it is mostly done by hands. Trust me if you can. It is easier for your hands to shape a basket made with twining than with plain weave. Once you have learned twining and shaping, it is a cinch to learn a plain weave, whereas the opposite is not true. So I have built this book around my "basic basket."

There are limitations in any undertaking. I believe that it is better to share what I can than to stop sharing because I don't know all there is to know. The number of techniques described in this book is limited to those related to the "basic basket." But, by the time you combine them and intermingle them with a variety of materials, shapes, and sizes, the possibilities are endless.

Learning is not always easy. There are times when I find I cannot learn a thing. Happily, there are also times when I am eager and willing to apply myself. And it often seems true to me that engaging in an activity that I have learned well, that I know how to do, at which I can hope to succeed, is one of the most rewarding things in life.

Only you, dear reader, know why you are reading this book. From this table by a sunny window after a December rain on my birthday, I have done what I can to share what I know. I sincerely wish you well.

# 1

# About Baskets in the Past

When I began weaving baskets and eventually began to think of myself as a basket weaver, one of the great fascinations that held me was the fact that it was a kind of lost art, almost no one else did it, and I had no competition to fear. That phenomenon didn't last long. I soon began teaching the people around me. And other people, in other places, began to learn as well.

Two facts never cease to amaze me, though. One is that basketry is the oldest craft ever practiced by man. It is probably precedent to pottery and is obviously the beginning of textile weaving. But it was not practiced only by primitive man. There is evidence that nearly every weave we know today dates back to before the written word. In light of that fact, the second is all the more remarkable: even unto this day, no one has invented a basket-making machine. Although baskets are sometimes made in a factory on a production line, even those are actually woven by hand. Just knowing that we still make baskets the same way our forebears did makes me smile inside as I weave.

Baskets were made in all parts of the world. They are mentioned as early as Genesis in the Bible. Roman gods were often depicted with baskets on their heads. Roman furniture, chariots, even helmets were of basketry. Roman soldiers on the English frontier made their temporary houses out of willows woven together. African homes are still constructed of basketry. Thor Heyerdahl told us about boats sailing around the world that were really just big baskets.

One of the most highly developed crafts anywhere in the world is American Indian basketry. The Indian woman wove baskets that were at once strong and graceful, and laid in careful patterns her poetry and dreams. George Wharton James, to whom I am indebted for knowledge and inspiration, went to live with the Indians in the early 1900's. He studied their way of life and wrote extensively, championing the life of the "aborigine" over the white people. White people, he said, were suffering from "Americanitis" with its grave symptoms of rush and greed.

He tells the story of an Indian widow with six children to feed who wove a basket with a picture of a burro eating at a trough. Since there was no such trough about, Mr. James asked her about the picture. Her reply was that she hoped one day to be able to afford such a trough so that her burro could eat "all same as rich man's beast."*

Mr. James founded a basket fraternity with some hundreds of members across the country. He published a quarterly, written mostly by himself, sold authentic aborigine basket patterns, and held competitions. Judging was based on the following ten points.

1. Suitability of the weave chosen
2. Form and shape of the basket
3. Execution of the stitch or weave
4. Use of materials, appropriateness, and harmony when used in combination
5. Fineness of material
6. Design
7. Color (On this item Mr. James commented, "Vegetable dyes are of greater value than any other." Of course one should feel at liberty to disagree.)
8. The finish: no loose ends, neatness of borders, corners, splicing and so on
9. Size in relation to intended use
10. General effect

An interesting article from the summer issue of 1904 told of and quoted from a lecture given at the Brooklyn Institute by Miss Helene Johnson. Miss Johnson, who had studied basketry with the Indians of Southern California and Hawaii, served as supervisor of basketry in the school system in and around Lowell, Massachusetts. The mate-

* The Basket, The Journal of the Basket Fraternity or Lovers of Indian Baskets and Other Good Things. Vol. II. No. 1. Jan. 1904; Poetry and Symbolism of Indian Basketry, by George Wharton James (Pasadena, California, 1904), p. 19.

rials she used included sweet grass, cedar bark, beach tree roots, seaweed, lemon lily leaves, cattail leaves, and wisteria fiber.

From her lecture: (The emphases are hers.)

First of all, the motive must be *found*, lit upon, born, not *sought*. The article must respond to a need, and its mould and ornament be produced not from a wish to please, but from a desire to express a certain real pleasure in the conceiver's mind; the joy that has come to him in the vision or sudden perceiving of some wonderful, lovely thing in nature; the deep emotion with which he has recognized the secret correspondence between the *form of things* and the *spirit of life*.

. . . Remember, too, that each squaw used but one or two kinds of weaves in all her lifetime, and do not ask to be made proficient in sixteen by one term of lessons!

In the southeastern highlands of America,* baskets are mostly woven of hickory and oak splits. In the 1930's they were valuable currency for poor farmers. The basket makers know where to cut the finest trees, to quarter, soak, pound, and split the wood to make baskets that will outlive their makers in strength and usefulness. There is poetry in a list of baskets named for their shape or their use, or sometimes for the family who wove them: round, flat, square, bowl, melon, hip, boat, jug, egg, tea, trinket, charcoal, lady, market, wall, work, flower, fruit, lunch, Rector, Purvis, and Moore.

A Mr. Eye of Kentucky maintained his family of sixteen, "including parents," by making and selling oak split baskets. He reckoned he'd made seven thousand. He'd begun as a lad and then he'd kept track for a long time.

There is also the story of the "famous" Dysart sisters, Lena and Flora, who supported themselves, in their seventies, by making honeysuckle baskets. They gathered the vine from their own land. In their own words:

We gather a quantity fifteen to twenty feet long in winter when the sap is down, wind them in rolls, fasten securely, and boil four hours. Remove from the pot, run each piece through a cloth to remove the bark, soak overnight in tub of water, rinse in two waters and hang in sunshine to dry. Then we whittle off each little knot with a sharp pocket knife and then we are ready for weaving.

* Eaton, A., *Handicrafts in the Southern Highlands*, Russell Sage Foundation (New York, 1934).

New England's basket tradition, learned from the Indians and brought from the old countries, is also mostly of oak splits. New Englanders added "ears" which enable the handle to move from side to side. An interesting evolution in New England produced the Nantucket Lightship Basket, so named because for a while the crews on lightships anchored as sentinels in Nantucket Sound made them on board ship to keep busy. The baskets have a turned wood bottom, wooden or cane staves and handle. They are woven of wood splits or cane with scrimshaw decorations and are now popular handbags commanding high prices.

The word "basket" is defined by Webster as "a receptacle made of interwoven osiers, cane, rushes, splints or other flexible material." A flautist I once met told me that the Swahili word for basket translates to "a house for little things."

Scholars seem to agree that the exact origin of the word "basket" is unclear. A brief study of the possibilities, however, yielded several things of interest.

Coffins and coffers are no longer associated with baskets, but at one time both were made of wickerwork. Both words are from the Latin *cophinus*, meaning a wicker basket. Canisters were once baskets, not tin boxes. *Canistra* is the Latin root. Another Roman basket called a *fiscus* and used for collecting tributes, has given us the words "fiscal" and "confiscate."

In England, basket making is an honored profession. For union membership the apprenticeship is five to seven years. The Basket Makers Company, or Craft Guild as it is now called, was established in 1569. The motto, established at that time for the guild, means what it seems to: "Lettan Us Luffer An Other."*

English basket vocabulary is beautiful. Weaving methods are known as "fitching, pairing, lapping, listing, randing and waling." A fish measure is called a "cran." A worker is "on the plank" when he works, as commonly the basket is held on an inclined board with an awl for ease in weaving the sides. There is "slath construction" and "slewing" and "slyping." But my favorite is "kindness." Kindness is used to describe the willingness or the cooperation of the willow

* H. H. Bobart, M.B.E., *Basket Work Through the Ages* (Oxford University Press, London, 1936).

rods. The rod one uses to do the weaving is known as the weaver. We also refer to the person doing the weaving as the weaver.

Surely if there is kindness in the weaver and the weaver is kind, the basket will prosper.

A small blue cask for rose petals.
It measures about four inches long.

# 2

# Words and Tools

BASIC BASKET—My choice of a center, weave, and border technique, which I believe to be a good way for a beginner to get a start.

BORDER—The top edge of the basket in which a rim is woven with the stakes or applied to the tops of the stakes.

BREAKING DOWN—Once the center is held together, breaking down is the process of separating the stakes, usually done in two or more stages.

CENTER—The center of the bottom. The beginning of the basket where all the stakes are held together.

STAKES—Also uprights, staves, warp. Those pieces that cross the bottom and go up the sides and into the border.

STROKE—One movement of one "weaver" by the hand of the person weaving.

TWINING—The name of the weave used in the basic basket. Twining has been used extensively by the Aleutian Islands Eskimos in grass baskets, socks, and mittens, sometimes more than fifty warp threads per inch. It is also used in Indian ceremonial blankets made of goats' wool and cedar bark.

UPSETT—The bottom edge of a basket, or the place where the stakes turn up. It also sometimes refers to the three or four rows of a heavier weave used to accomplish the upsett.

WEAVE—The weft or fill. Any of several ways to fill in the framework provided by the stakes, and to shape the basket. The "weaver" is the material used to fill in the framework.

## Tools

The most important tool of the basket weaver is a pair of *willing hands*. Then you will need something for *soaking:* a pot, a basin, a kitchen sink, or a bathtub. In the summer I take a basin outside. In the winter I like to work by the Franklin stove. The cut-off scraps make excellent kindling. Sometimes I add a little dish-washing soap to the water to make it smell nice. Warm water is more comfortable so I usually use it. If you have hard water, you may want to add water softener or gather rainwater.

For *cutting,* I use kitchen shears. Any strong scissors will do. I also use a pair of electricians' side cutters. These are clippers that have the short, strong cutting edges set off to one side. If you do a lot of basketry they might prove worth the investment but they are not essential. They are available at hardware stores for a few dollars. Their advantage is in trimming close on the finished basket. They also offer an extra leverage that makes cutting easier on fairly large reeds or vines. On *very* large reed I also cut by whittling with a sharp paring knife.

For *pinching,* you can use your teeth, pliers, the spot where the two handles of a pair of scissors meet, a hammer and the edge of a table or board, or a pair of round-nose pliers.

As for *work space,* I quote my young son, "Another man's poison is another man's good." One book I read said in effect, "Don't think that you can work in the corner of your kitchen because the material takes up a lot of space." Pshaw! I've been working in the corner of my kitchen most of the time I've been working, and even though my kitchen does sometimes resemble the jungle where the reed began its life, we've never eaten reeds instead of spaghetti. I'm sure you can solve the question for yourself. It is helpful to hang the reed from a high hook or nail, or over the corner of an open door. The actual weaving can be done on a flat table top, chair seat, or just held in your hands. For very large baskets, I often find it helpful to work the basket upside down, with the bottom of the basket over an up-turned pail or a pot. The Indian women used a tree stump.

In case a stake breaks in the middle of your work, or if you are making handles, you will want something in the nature of a steel knitting needle to slip down into the weaving to make a space for a new stake or the core of the handle. An awl, a bodkin, a shishkebab skewer, a chopstick, or great patience will do the trick.

If you gather your own materials, you will need stout shears to cut them and a large pot to boil them in. A pot twelve inches across or more is good. Although you can fit more vines in a larger pot and the water boils away less quickly, a large pot of water is heavy. Most vines are not poisonous so you can use one of your cooking pots.

If you dye your own colors, beware of brass or iron pots as they affect the hues. Also some dyes *are* poisonous so I strongly recommend setting aside a separate pot. You can boil vines in it but not your Saturday stew.

Once in a while a clip-type clothespin will come in handy to hold something in place. If you make roped handles, you will want a penknife or paring knife.

I'll be talking more about these supplies and tools later on. For now, let's make a basket.

# 3

# Basic Basket

The basic basket has three parts, the *center* which is the beginning, the *weave* which includes shaping the basket, and the *border* which is the finish.

You will need:

1. Reed
2. A basin or sink to soak it in
3. A pair of scissors (or something that cuts)
4. A general idea of shape and size (this first basket will be approximately five inches across the bottom and four inches up the sides and somewhat bowl-shaped)
5. A pair of willing hands

*Reed* is also known as cane, rattan, center cane, pulp cane, kindergarten reed, handicraft reed, and sometimes wicker. Reed is the easiest material to learn with. I ask that you begin with it.

Reed must be purchased from a craft store or through the mail (see mail supply list at the end of this chapter). It is sold by the pound in graduated sizes, #1 through #12. For your first basket I recommend that you buy one pound each of sizes #2 and #4. You will need the larger #4 for stakes and the smaller #2 to weave with. You might start with #1 and #3, or #2 and #3, or #1 and #4, but do not start with any larger sizes. Wait until you have made a few baskets. (If your craft store does not carry reed in the exact size you want, ask them to order it — or use one of the mail-order suppliers.)

We are so accustomed to seeing reed used in commercial baskets that we tend to think of it as a factory product. It does come to us from a factory, but it starts out in the jungles of the South Pacific islands. My guess is that Tarzan might have swung on it, but perhaps he swung in Africa. Reed is a member of the palm family, and actually several varieties are used in basketry, though I have no way of knowing which variety it is that is sold here.

A reed harvest takes several days. Slashing through thick jungles, wearing heavy leather gloves to protect them from the huge thorns on the reed, the men cut the plants about three feet above the ground. This allows the plant to produce another growth, a process that takes seven years. The vines are left hanging, as the natives work on into the jungle. When they return a few days later, the outer bark has dried and come loose, and the thorns have shriveled, so that in pulling down the vines the bark and thorns are removed. The vines are cut into lengths of 15 to 30 feet, coiled and sent by boat to a warehouse plant. There they are sorted for size and quality and given a sulphur bath. The sulphur acts as both a bleach and an insecticide. The vines are sent to factories around the world where machine processes produce chair cane, from the inner bark, and the various shapes and sizes of center cane or reed that are used in other basket weaving.

When you have the reed at home and are ready to begin, undo all the bonds of each coil except the three or four that hold the strands together.

Loop a piece of string around the reed as shown and hang it up

somewhere. Then it is easy to pull out one strand at a time. Remember that reed is a plant. Sometimes pieces of it are stringy and full of whiskers. Take the time to select the pieces you want to use.

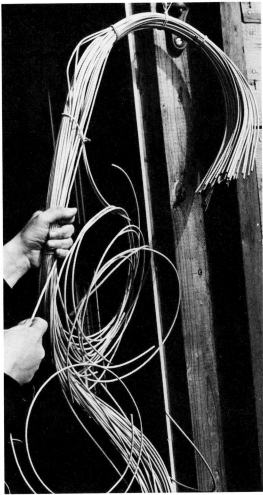

Pull six single strands of #2, the smaller size, one at a time and coil each strand. This is done by wrapping it round and round in a small circle as you would a garden hose or a length of rope on a boat. Then wrap the end three or four times around through the center to hold it together. This makes it easy to take one piece at a time when you are weaving.

Put the coils in water to soak.

Cut ten 20-inch lengths of #4 and put them also in to soak. You need not measure exactly. The error factor may be as large as an inch, but better too long than too short. Twenty inches is about a hand's width longer than a common kitchen chair seat.

About soaking: I soak the reed at my own convenience. You need not set the kitchen timer. There is a rule of thumb, however, for maximum protection of the reed. Size #1 through size #4 should soak only as long as five to ten minutes. Sizes #5 and up can stay in the water up to twenty minutes. I never think about it and probably I often soak my reed longer than necessary. Once your hands have become familiar with handling reed you will know when it has been soaked enough.

A brief preview of the weave. It is called *twining,* or sometimes "pairing." I call it twining because it is done with two weavers which twine around each other as they weave the basket.

Take one coil of #2 out of the water. You are going to fold it and use its two halves as the two weavers. However, you do not want to fold it exactly in half, or both weavers will run out at the same time and place on the basket, causing two splices to be necessary next to each other. So find a point on the strand of #2 anywhere off center by a few inches. Pinch that spot with your thumbnail, between the handles of your scissors, with a pair of pliers, or with your teeth. Pinching will help it fold without breaking. Fold it at that spot.

If it breaks anyway when you fold it, I would guess that you have a punk piece of reed, have hit a punk spot, or haven't soaked the reed enough. Chances are that you can use it anyway, unless it breaks clean through. If it does, put it aside and try another piece.

You have a loop and two weavers now.

If you are right-handed, you will be weaving with your right hand in a clockwise direction, so hold up your left hand. If you are left-

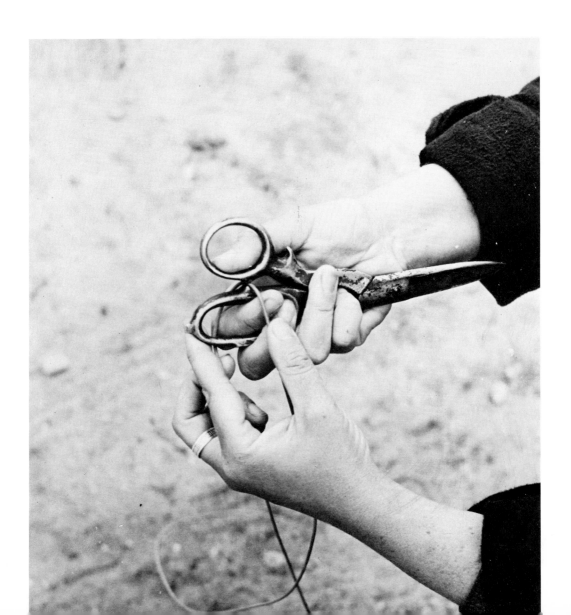

handed you will be weaving with your left hand in a counterclockwise direction, so hold up your right hand.

To try out the weave, pretend that your fingers are the basket you
are working on. Loop the fold in the weaver around your thumb. Have
your palm facing you and the two weavers trailing off to the back.
For now the two weavers must always trail off to the back.

Consider the direction you will be going. *Take the weaver that is farther behind. Bring it forward through the next space,* between your thumb and first finger. *It will cross on top of the other weaver.* Then *take it back through the next space,* between your index and middle fingers.

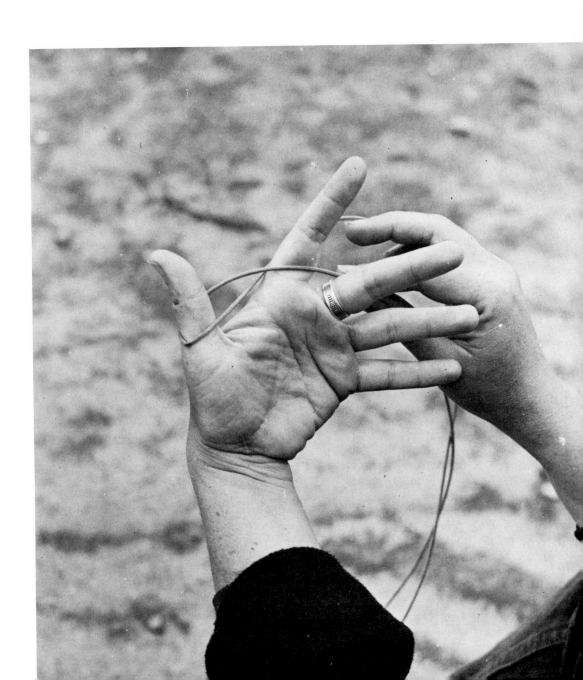

The action of bringing the weaver that is farther behind forward and then taking it back through the next space is called a *stroke*. I have chosen this description very carefully. It will help you if you think of it in these words when you are doing the weave on your basket for the first time.

Now, you see, you have left the other weaver behind, so you do

a stroke with it. *Bring it forward* between your index and middle fingers, *crossing on top of the other weaver, and take it back again in the next space.* So it goes, stroke after stroke. Do it until you run out of fingers. Then slip the weaver off your fingers and you will see why it is called twining weave.

Now we can begin the basket. Set the weaver aside for a minute. Take the ten 20-inch pieces of #4 out of the water. These we will call *stakes*.

Place five stakes vertically and five horizontally, crossing on top, or in front of, the verticals.

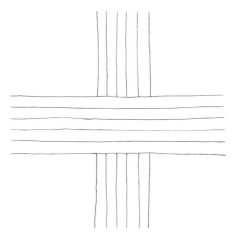

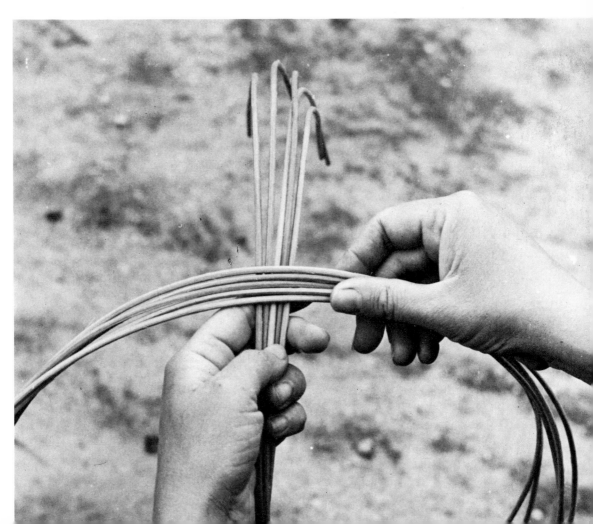

Now if you are left-handed, you will have to, as you do so often in a right-handed world, translate the following into a counterclockwise direction.

The first two rounds involve lashing these two groups of five together. After you have done it a few times it will make sense, so this first time do not worry about remembering specific moves.

Untwist your weaver and loop the fold around the top group of five, just as you did around your thumb.

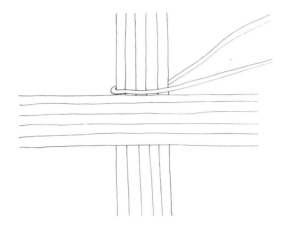

Now you have two weavers, one crossing in front of the top group of stakes and one crossing behind. Fold the back weaver down in front of the horizontal group of five.

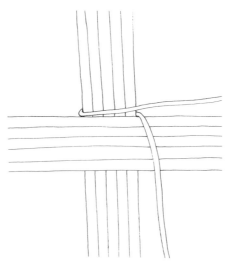

Now fold the other weaver, the one that crossed in front, around and down in back of the same group of five horizontal stakes.

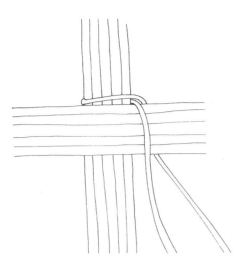

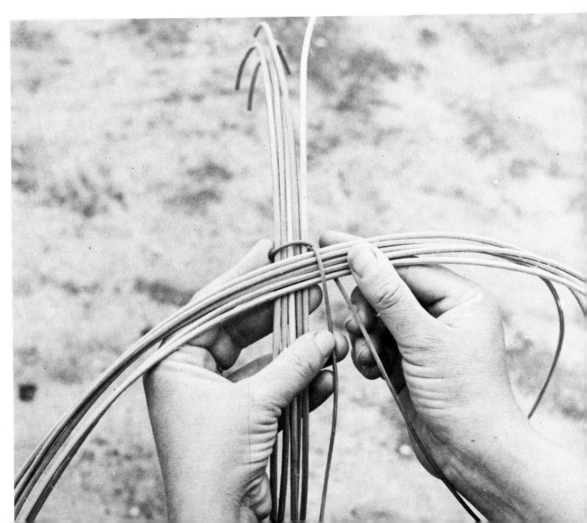

Fold the front weaver across in back of the lower group of vertical stakes.

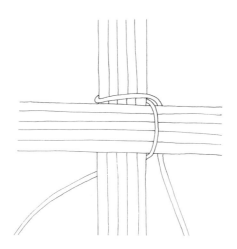

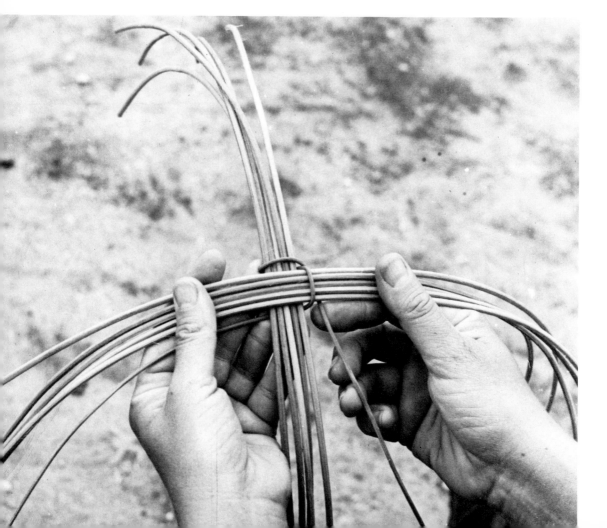

Then fold the other weaver across in front of that same group of stakes.

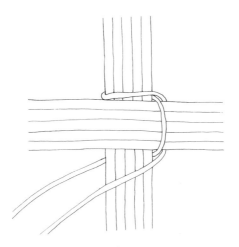

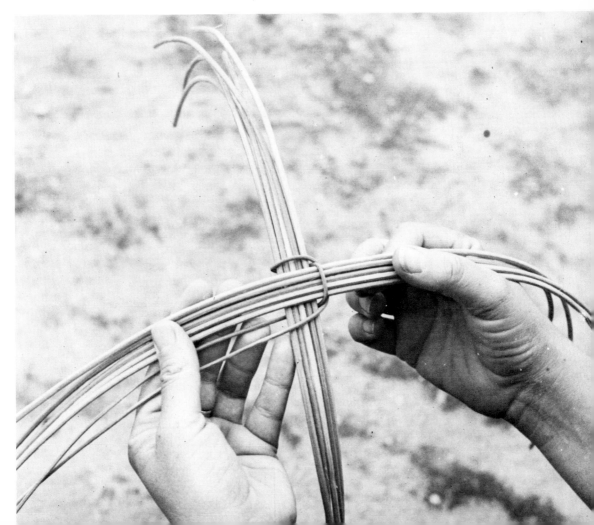

Take the weaver that went behind the bottom group of stakes and fold it up in front of the remaining group of horizontal stakes.

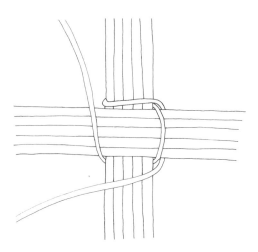

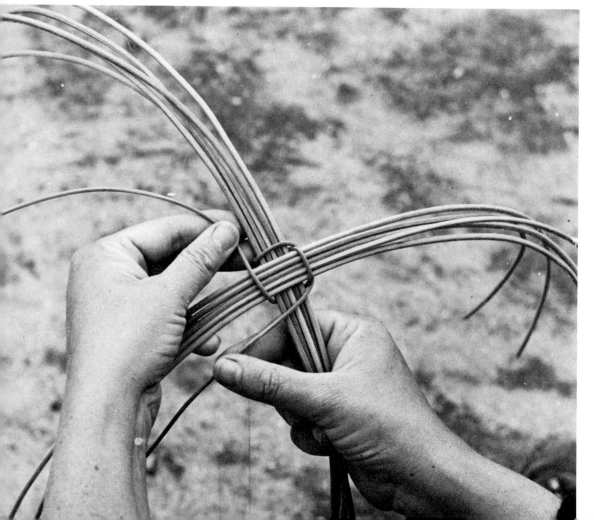

Now fold the other up behind them.

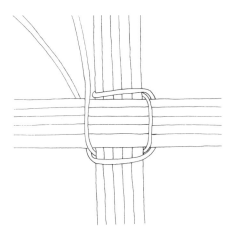

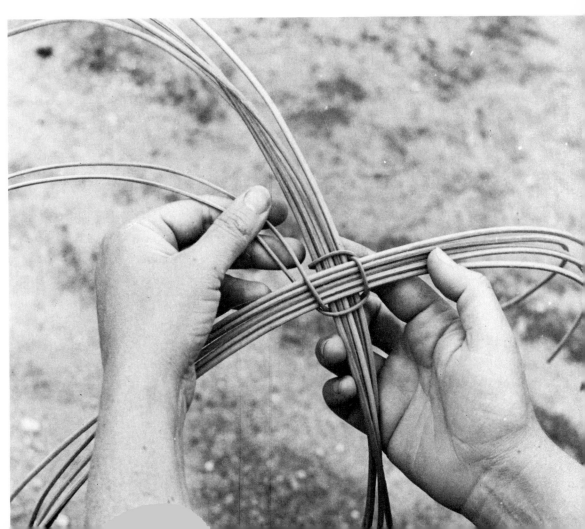

Go all the way around again in like manner, following the drawings and the photos.

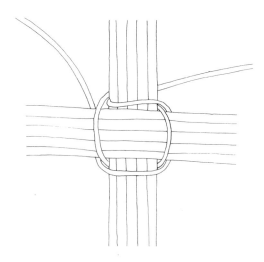

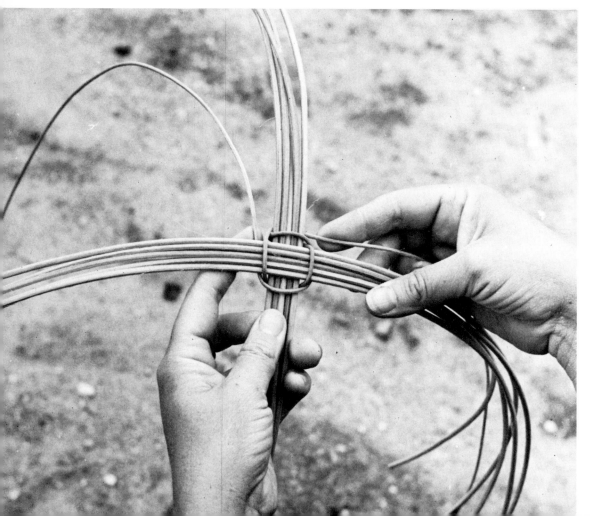

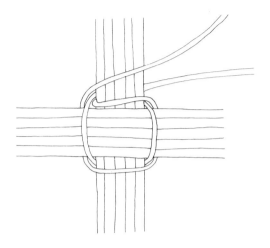

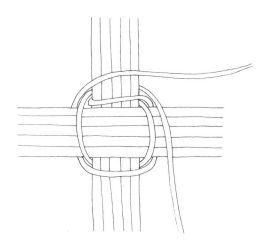

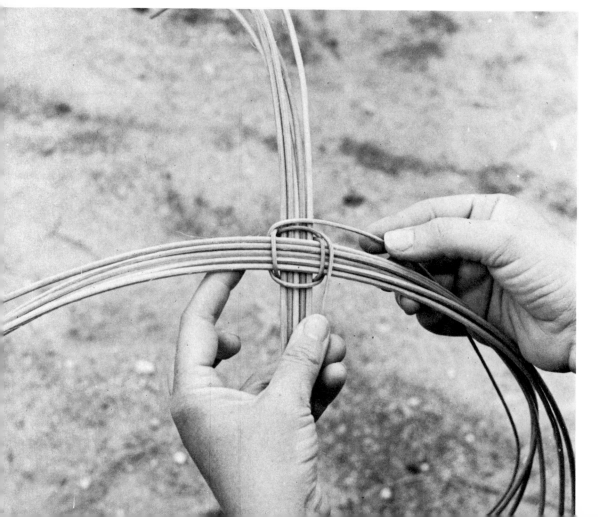

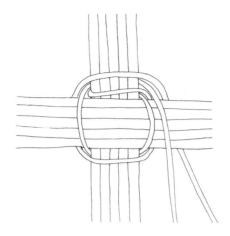

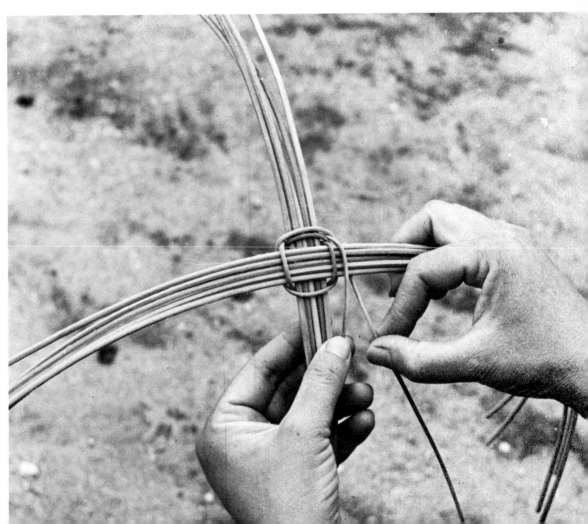

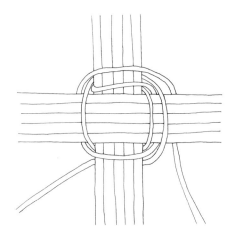

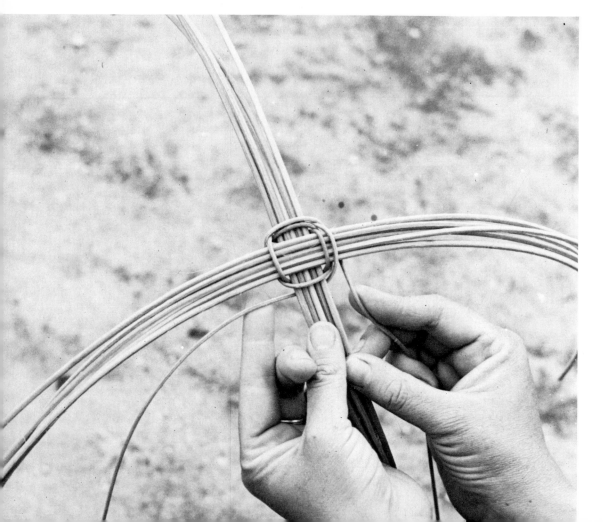

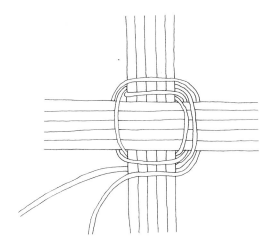

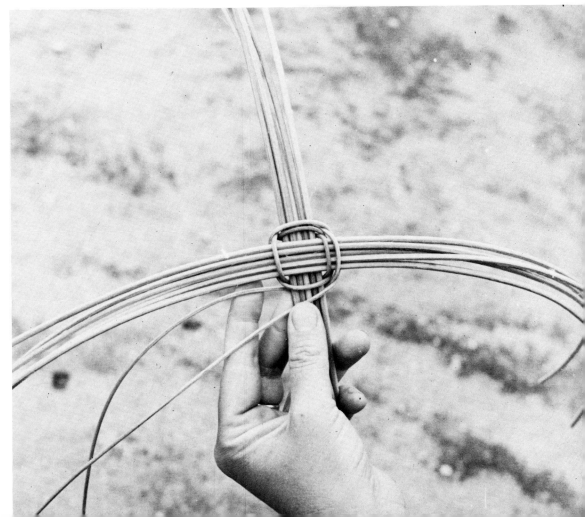

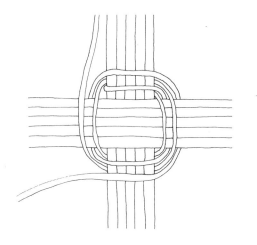

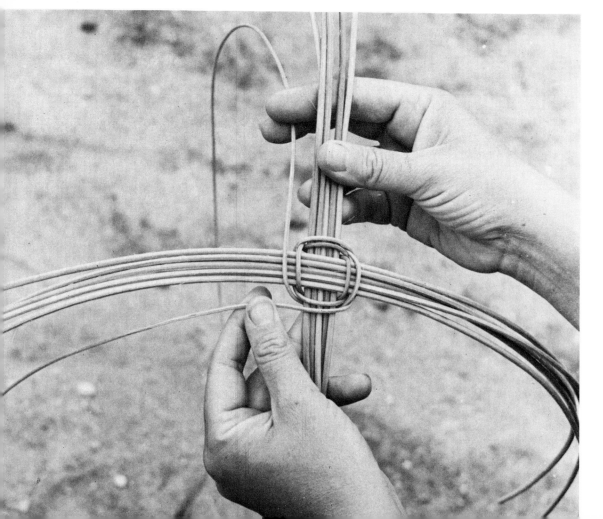

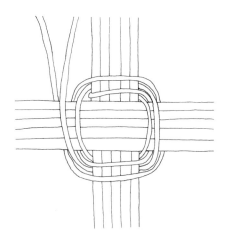

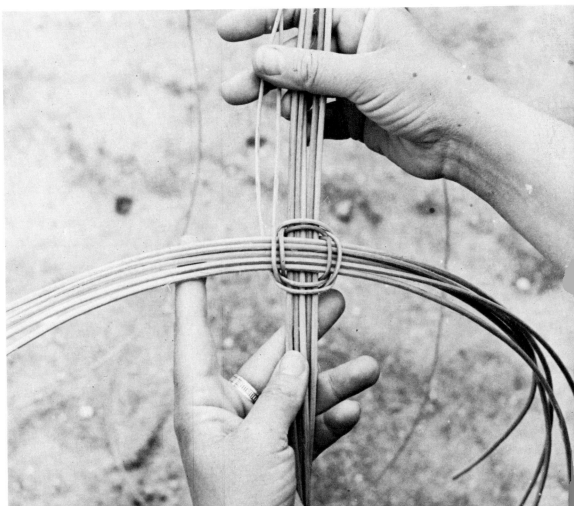

## Breaking Down

Please forgive the awful pun. Breaking down a basket is a two-stage operation that separates the groups of five stakes into single stakes. Once you have done it my way, you may design your breakdowns in any combination you like. The breakdown also serves another purpose. It extends the circle of weaving so that it is big enough for the weaving to fit between single stakes.

It is at this time also that twining is begun. For each stroke, *take the weaver that is farther behind, bring it forward, crossing on top of the other weaver, and take it back through the next space.*

Stage one: Each group of five will be divided into two, one, and two. Go around twice.

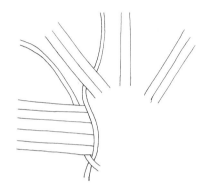

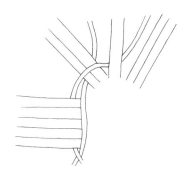

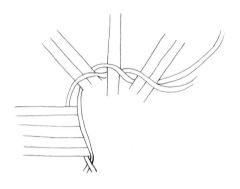

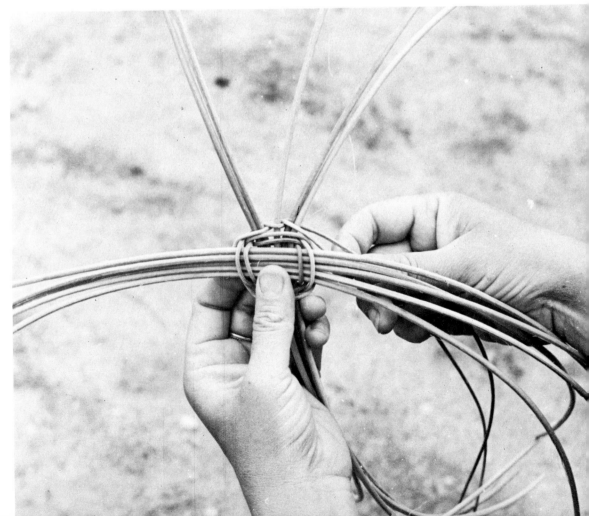

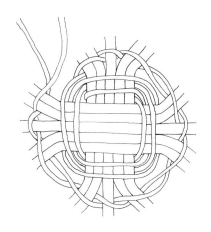

Stage two: Separate and weave around each stake by itself.

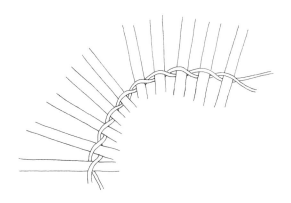

## Splicing

Splicing is done by weaving the weaver until it can't possibly go another stroke, and then sticking the end of a new weaver alongside of it for half a stroke, and proceeding to weave with the new one (see below).

Here you might consider the idea of a "right" and "wrong" side to the weaving. In most instances in basketry there are no right and wrong sides. If you are making a basket to hold silks or wools you will want to leave all rough ends on the outside. If you have a basket with a lid perhaps you might leave them inside. Splices are acceptable in baskets however. They do not seem as obvious on a finished basket as they do during the process of weaving.

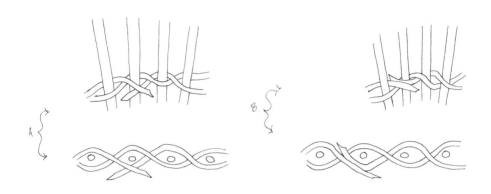

## Upsetting

Upsetting is the transition from the bottom to the sides. In the basic basket it is accomplished by turning each stake up in the angle you want it, or slightly sharper, and then weaving around it. You do not

have to hold the stakes all the way around, but I did in the basket photographed. If you want a very abrupt upsett, it is helpful to pinch each stake at the point at which you want it to turn.

Do the best you can to make the shape that you want. But I always

say, "Don't tell anyone else what shape you are going to make." Your first basket probably won't turn out to be exactly the shape you intended, but that is not important this time. It is by doing that your hands will learn how to shape the weaving. That is one reason I

chose twining as the first weave to learn. It is the best, in my opinion, for letting your hands learn the process of shaping.

If after four or five rounds you have not upsett the stakes at all, take out those rounds and try again with a little more conviction.

Once you have upsett, continue weaving the sides until they measure about four inches, or until you have about six inches of standing stakes left. If you want the sides to flare out, push each stake a little farther away from the one before it on each stroke. If you want the sides to come in push the stakes closer together.

Note: If a stake breaks anywhere in the process of weaving, either go on as if it hadn't or cut it clean at the break and insert a new stake with the help of an awl or knitting needle.

*The Border*

Soak the basket once more, about five minutes. Since baskets float, you will have to contrive some way to make the stakes stay under water. The part of the stakes that need to soak is from the last couple of rows of weaving to the tips.

This border is called a closed border. It is done in two rounds. First trim off any excess weaver. (Do not trim stakes yet.) Then pinch each stake at the top of the weaving.

Round one: Beginning anywhere and with any stake, and going in either direction, lay the first stake down parallel to the weaving on the outside of the stake next to it and to the inside of the next.*

* The basic border may also be done backwards, i.e. *Round one:* Going in either direction lay the first stake to the inside of the stake next to it and back to the outside of next stake. *Round two:* Going in same direction as round one, beginning with any stake, lift up the next stake and poke the one before it in the space thus formed.

This border may be easier, depending on the shape of your basket and the length of stakes left over. If you have had trouble with either way please try the other.

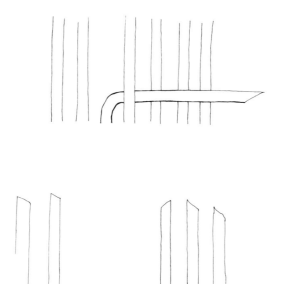

Do this all the way around. As you take the next stake to its place it will hold down the one before it. The final stake must be poked through the space left between the first and second stakes.

Round two: On the second round you tuck the stakes back to the outside where they will be trimmed off. Going in the same direction, beginning with any stake, lift up the next stake and poke the end of the first stake through the space created.

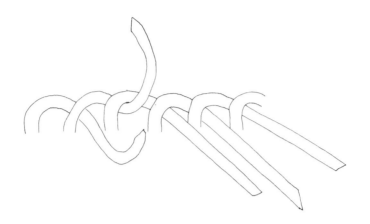

Now you may want to tighten up the border by pushing and pulling a little. Then trim the ends off a little beyond the stake that is holding each in its place. Look carefully to see which that is. When I was still new at basket weaving I had a tendency to trim my borders too short, which resulted in their popping out. I hope my telling you of it will save you from the same experience.

## SOURCES OF BASKETRY MATERIALS

H. H. Perkins Co., 10 South Bradley Road, Woodridge, Connecticut 06525. Free booklet and price list.

Peerless Rattan and Reed Mfg. Co., Inc., 97 Washington St., New York, New York 10006. Free booklet and price list.

Cane and Basket Supply Co., 1283 South Cochran Ave., Los Angeles, California 90019. Free samples and price list.

Creative Handweavers, P.O.B. 26480, Los Angeles, California 90026.

Naturalcraft, 2199 Bancroft Way, Berkeley, California 94704. Catalog and samples $.50.

WARP, Woof and Potpourri, 514 North Lake Ave., Pasadena, California 91101. Catalog and samples $.50.

The Yarn Depot, Inc., 545 Sutter St., San Francisco, California 94102.

The Yarn Loft, Upstairs, 1442 Camino Del Mar, Del Mar, California 92014.

Sax Arts and Crafts, 207 North Milwaukee St., Milwaukee, Wisconsin 53202. Catalog $.50.

J. C. Larson Co., 7330 N. Clark St., Chicago, Illinois 60626.

Dick Blick Art Materials, P.O.B. 1267, Galesburg, Illinois 61401.

CCM Arts and Crafts, Inc., 9520 Baltimore Ave., College Park, Maryland 20740.

I really like this picture. The basket is about 25 inches across. The bottom is made on spline, which is really meant for chair caning. I used #6 as both stakes and weavers. You can see that the stakes have been inserted.

# 4
# Other Basket Materials

Baskets have traditionally been made out of materials that are handy. The meaning of basket weaving has changed with time, as well as the availability of materials. Your own choices of materials will come from your understanding of the meaning of the activity and from what you can get. The list below, of course, reflects my meaning and my environment. I hope that it will inspire you to try other things as well.

*Reed*, also known as rattan or cane, is a vine of the palm family (see chapter 3).

*Raffia*, also of the palm family, is an inner layer of leaf. It looks like grass skirt material and may be. It is available in craft shops and by mail from the same sources as reed. Raffia is sold by the pound, and one pound will make several small baskets. It can be bought in colors, but it is easily dyed at home with either packaged or vegetable dyes. Raffia must be handled gently as it splits easily. I usually hang up a bunch through a loop when I am using it, so that one strand can be pulled at a time.

*Hong Kong Grass* is a twisted oriental sea grass that can be purchased from most of the same places as reed. It smells nice and looks pretty. Since it has little structural strength of its own, I use it together with reed or other vine. A problem with Hong Kong Grass is that the ends untwist when it is cut, so you must sew them together with needle and thread.

*Fibre Rush* and *Fibre Splints,* also available at most basket supply places, are made from paper to look like rush and splints for chair seating. In my opinion they look like paper, but they are interesting to use in basket weaving.

*Wire*, single-strand thin copper or other metal wire, available in hardware stores, is fun and offers its own dimensions when used in basketry. A pair of round-nosed pliers is useful when working with it. Be aware when you buy it that some wires rust.

*Yarn* and *Twine* of all sorts can be used alone or with other materials. Making baskets is a good way to use up scraps. If you are making your first basket with yarn alone — that is, yarn (or twine) for both stakes and weavers — the stakes do not have to be larger than the weavers. Use the thickest yarn you can for learning. Work on a table or board. You might find it helpful to use thumbtacks or pins to hold the work. The main difference with these soft materials is that the structure of the basket is formed by the weaving rather than by the stakes. As you weave, stop every little while to push the weaving in tightly against itself. This is the same thing as beating the filler on a loom. The shape of this sort of basket is determined by the amount of warp threads or stakes. New stakes must be added as you weave for as long as you want the bottom to stay flat.* I usually add them at will but you can count and devise a system to keep them regular if you like. When you stop adding stakes the sides will begin to turn up as you weave. I splice by tying a square knot. Knots are generally considered bad practice in basketry, but they work in this case. When the basket is finished you can untie them and hide the ends in the weaving with the help of a crochet hook. The simple closed border of the basic basket is very effective with yarn.

*Fabric* cut into strips makes interesting and durable pouches and such. Cut any fabric into half-inch strips or whatever width you like. If the fabric ravels it can be cut on the bias or with pinking shears. Strips about one yard long or less are the easiest to handle. Splice by sewing on a new strip when the old one runs out.

*Old baskets* usually wear out first on the bottoms. It is often possible to soak them well and take them apart to salvage some of the material to make a small basket.

*Corn husks* are better suited to chair seats, dolls, and coil basketry than the work covered in this book. But you might have a use for them and I happen to know how to prepare them so I am including them here anyway. Harvest them at the same time as you want to eat

---

* See page 92 for notes on how to add stakes.

the corn. Discard the dark green outer husks. Supermarket corn often comes with the light green husks left on. Those are the ones to use. Spread them out in a dry place to dry for about a week. If you want them to stay green, dry them in the dark. If you want them to bleach, put them in a sunny spot. They can be dyed. When you are ready to use the husks, cut off the curled end with scissors, and split them to whatever width you want.

*Blackberry Brambles.* When I was just beginning to make baskets, I read the direction for cooking honeysuckle vine, quoted elsewhere, and was inspired to try it, so I set off with my two-year-old son to find some honeysuckle. Two-year-olds do not make rapid progress on grown-up errands and we kept tripping and getting scratched. Soon I gave up, and gathered the tough thorny stuff that was tripping and scratching us. At home, following the honeysuckle directions, I wove the vines into rustic little nests. I later found out that they were brambles and are a time-honored weaving material.

Brambles can be used with the bark left on or stripped off. Here is the recipe: Gather the vines in the fall or winter when the sap is down. Wear heavy leather work gloves. If the vines are very long cut them into workable lengths as you gather them. I usually gather 25 to 50 lengths at a time. Then, working outdoors or someplace easy to sweep up, hold one end of a vine firmly and pull it through a gloved hand. Now run it through in the other direction. One way takes off the thorns, the other the leaves. Coil the vines, in bunches of three or four, into coils that will fit your pot. Put the coils in the pot and cover them with water. Bring the water to a boil and simmer the vines for four hours. When you remove the pot from the heat, let the vines stand in the water overnight. Rinse well, strip the bark if you choose to by peeling, and the vines are ready for weaving. Or you can hang them up to dry, still in coils, and store them for later use. They will keep indefinitely. When you are ready to use the dried coils, soak them about five minutes in warm water. Brambles should be boiled within twenty-four hours after cutting.

*Honeysuckle vine* is wonderful to work with. The bark practically peels itself after it has been boiled, or you can leave it on if you want a shaggy effect. Stripped honeysuckle vine is a soft green color that fades in a short time to off white and will take dye. Gather it by cutting in the fall or winter. You needn't wear gloves, but don't try to pull it; honeysuckle is tough. You can leave the leaves on for now. Coil it to fit your pot, cover with water, boil, and simmer for four hours. Turn off the heat and let the coil stand overnight. Rinse and use, or hang to let dry and then store. The vine needs to be soaked only a few minutes when you are ready to use it. After you uncoil it, strip off the bark and the leaves with a soft cloth. You will perhaps notice a difference or two in this recipe from the one I quote in the first chapter. This is the way I do it and it seems to work well. I would encourage anybody to do whatever works for him. One of my students made a honeysuckle basket last summer out of fresh-cut green honeysuckle without boiling. It is a fine little basket and still functional.

*Raspberry runners, wisteria, clematis, grapevines, English ivy, Virginia creeper,* and *coralberry runners.* There are probably many more. They can all be processed as you would honeysuckle.

*Willow* is specifically cultivated for basket weaving in many places. It is the strongest yet lightest of materials. A friend of mine just back from a visit to Europe went to visit a basket hermit somewhere in the mountains of France. He showed her his willow patch. He had several rows planted close together so they would grow tall. He had ways of harvesting it at several times of year to produce different colors. I don't know his secrets. But if you have access to a willow tree or pussy willows, you can gather the withes or the young shoots. If you gather them in the spring, soak them for a while until they are supple. If you gather them in the fall or winter, boil or steam them in a canning kettle. The bark can be peeled before or after soaking or boiling, or left on. Split willow rods are sometimes called skeins.

*Cattails* have long been used for rush seating. Where I live, on the east coast, I have not been able to make them work. I understand that the salt winds may have something to do with that. But if you live inland and want to try cattail leaves, gather the leaves when full grown but still green. Dry in the shade a few days. Pull off the rib down the center and throw it away and soak the leaves a few minutes. Use them right away. They can also be dyed.

*Red cedar bark,* from a fallen tree or log. Soak several weeks (in a stream perhaps) to remove the outer bark. Then peel off the inner bark in strips. Scrape with a paring knife or such to make smooth.

*Grasses.* I have never done this but I pass it on for possible experimentation. Gather enough grasses to make a bundle about the size of a woman's waist. I think that you should think in terms of a stout woman. Wrap the bunch tightly in burlap and put in a cool dark place for ten days. Each day open the bundle and turn the grasses to expose the stems equally to the air. This will toughen the inner leaves. The grasses turn yellow. After ten days strip each bundle to the inner leaves. Split the stems with your thumbnail and pull out the inner leaf (8 to 12 inches long). These become the weavers. The outers are the stakes. Sort both by length, hang them in the sun to bleach and dry (about three days), and wrap them in paper to store. Soak them a few minutes to use. This is the method of the Attu women of Alaska. They make very finely woven large baskets using almost exactly the same method as the basic basket.

Brambles growing in the sand where a new road had been cut through the moors. As they grow they seem to me to be weaving themselves into baskets to hold the earth together.

# 5

# Basic Variations

I sometimes work as an actress. A director once told me this: "An actor's two most important tools are the total of his experience and the total of his imagination." Once you have made a basket you have had some basketry experience. The skill and dexterity you wish to develop will take care of itself, I believe. Human beings, it seems to me, have an unquenchable drive to do a little better each time. Your imagination is what provides the spice that makes you want to try again. Here are some ideas from my experiences and my imagination which I offer to yours.

*Size.* You can use as few as two stakes crossing two in the center and as many as ten crossing ten. Now you will want to ask the question that has worried me as author-authority from the beginning of my work. It goes something like this, "How do I know how many stakes to use?" It means more than that, too. It means, "How do you design a basket?" It is easy enough to conceive of a lovely shape and size. And it is easy enough to believe that in time you will be able to make a basket that looks something like the size and shape that you imagined. But how do you *know* how to make that shape and size the right strength for itself and its function? I have haunted the works of my predecessors in vain. They seem to have avoided the issue altogether, or cleverly skirted it by sticking to basket recipes. I decided to meet the challenge head on. Perhaps someday there will be a basket building code that will say, "Any basket over 4 inches and under 6 inches must use at least four #4's, three #5's, or two #6's for each 2-inch span on the circumference." For here and now, dear reader, there is no simple answer. You must try what you think will work and if it doesn't, modify that basket a little, then try again for the original design. But that is the nice thing about making baskets today. The investment in each one is very small both in time and money. So each mistake can be used as a step ahead. In England, where basket making is a profession, the apprenticeship is seven years. I have been working only four years and most of my baskets are "mistakes." I do not want to become professional. I thoroughly enjoy the process of starting with an idea and then working in co-operation with the material and the laws of gravity and such, letting a basket evolve.

The only practical consideration I can offer to the dilemma is this: While you are weaving the base, the stakes are being held farther and farther apart by the weaving as you go. There will come a point on any base when they are too far apart to insure a strong border. If you can imagine the border while weaving the base, and stop to upsett before you get to that point, you may save some time and embarrassment.

You may also use other sizes of reed. Or try other shapes of reed which give different textures. Keep in mind that most of the time, "the weaver should never master the stakes." You may use all one size of reed, using perhaps two pieces for each stake.

*Lids.* A lid is really just an upside down basket. Some care must be taken to have it look as though it belongs to the basket under it.

*Covered bottles* are not as hard to make as you'd think. In fact they are quite easy. If you have a bottle cutter there is no end to the fun possible.

*Other Materials.* You can weave yarn, string, twine, seaweed, grasses, beads, and shells in with reed. Use your imagination to find other materials.

*Flat Bottoms.* Many of my students have been anxious to have a basket that sits squarely on a table. For myself I enjoy casual baskets. But if you want a flat base here are four suggestions:

1. While weaving the base, work on the corner of a table to give yourself leverage and a flat surface. Make the weaver move around the stakes and keep the stakes flat.
2. Do the split center shown in the next chapter.
3. Crown the center up a little, as you weave the first few rows. Then flatten out the next few rows.

4. Add four beads (or three will do) just before the upsett to give the basket feet.

## Wooden Bases

Pre-cut bases are often available where reed is sold. They have holes drilled so one need only insert stakes and weave up the sides to make a basket. For anyone who finds the basic basket difficult, wooden bases may be the answer. It is also possible, of course, to make your own bases. They can be any shape. My young son makes them from heavy cardboard, punching holes with a hammer and nails. He uses reed as the stakes but he likes to weave with yarn and paint designs on the base. Stakes can be glued into the base holes. They can also be inserted as below.

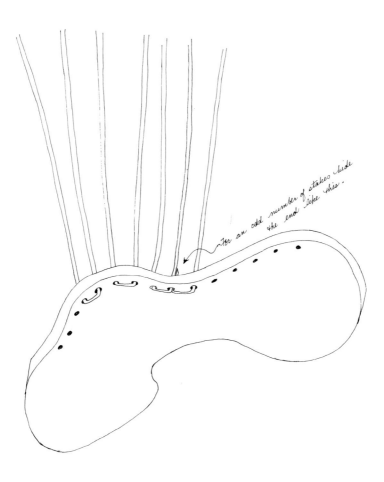

For an odd number of stakes hide the end like this.

Or, you can make a foot border. Cut stakes each long enough for the sides and *two* borders. Insert the stakes right on through the holes and weave a border on the bottom. Then turn it over and weave up the sides.

When you use a wooden base, be careful about getting it wet. Wood will stain, warp, and even split when wet. The base can be painted or shellacked before weaving.

I would like to suggest a good project for anyone working with children. The basic basket is not too hard for a child of ten or older. Still, you may want to use wooden or cardboard bases to save time or to save yourself trouble. Use bases and reed stakes or basic basket bases, and then have the children collect and process some local hedgerow material and weave their baskets from these.

# 6

# Weaves

At our house, baskets hang from the beams overhead. When I sit down, I invariably look up. There is something restful about the repetition of any weave. Each one has its own texture and that varies with different materials. So I hope you enjoy experimenting with some of these weaves.

*In and Out:* Also called randing, over-and-under, tabby weave.

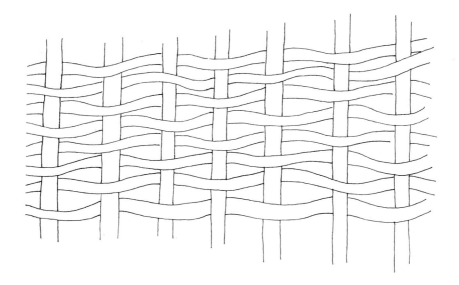

This weave can be done round and round on an *odd* number of stakes. An odd number of stakes can be arrived at in two ways. One way is to add a "bye" stake or half stake. When cutting stakes for the basket, cut one about three inches longer than half the length of the other stakes. Cut one end of this stake at a slant. When you are ready to break down, insert the pointed end alongside any other stake, with the help of a knitting needle if necessary.

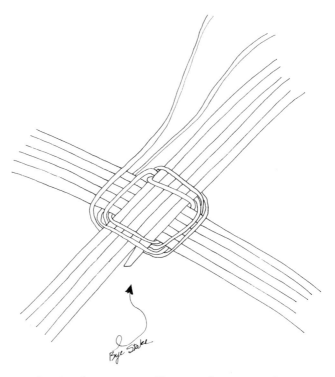

Another way is simply to cut off one of your stakes before the breakdown, thus giving you an odd number.

The in and out weave can also be worked on an even number of stakes by using the following trick to make it work row after row. At the beginning of the second round, and each round thereafter, go over two stakes, then go on with the weave. This spot where you go over two, moves over one stake each round, making a spiral up the side of the basket.

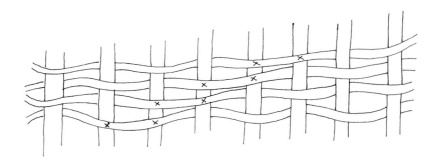

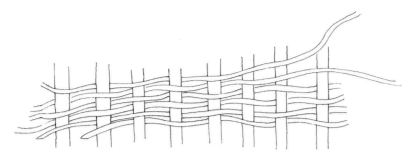

*Chasing* is the same weave done with two weavers, one after the other. The first weaver does one round in and out, then the second weaver does a round of out and in.

For designs using in and out weave, try natural stakes with colored weavers; bands of colored weavers; natural weavers on colored stakes; or chasing with the second weaver of a different color.

In and out can also be done with two or more weavers used together. Then it is called *Slewing.* Don't let the weavers twist together.

*Over Two and Under One:* Also called Rib Randing and Japanese Weave. It can be done on any number of stakes not divisible by three. For example: The basic basket center of five stakes crossing five stakes yields twenty stakes, which is not evenly divisible by three.

*Colonial Weave:* Over two and under two, can be done on any number of stakes *not* divisible by four.

a) Stakes divisible by four with a remainder of two: change the weave by going in back of one stake when you start the second row. You will understand what I mean by that when you get there.
b) Stakes divisible by four with a remainder of three. This makes a heavy coil slanting to the right.

c) Stakes divisible by four with a remainder of one. The coil slants to the left.

*Packing:* Any time you want to vary the height of the sides of a basket or the base, for shape or design effects, you can build up sections by packing. The illustration shows the over-and-under weave, but packing can be done in any weave and for any distance.

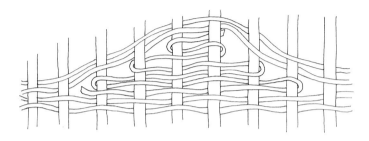

*Twining* is the "basic basket" weave. (It is also called "pairing.") To vary it, use two colors on an odd number of stakes to make spirals. Two colors on an even number of stakes will yield vertical stripes.

*Three Rod Wale:* This is done the same way as twining but with three weavers, each going over two and under one. It is easier than it sounds. Each stroke is just the same as twining. Keeping the three weaver ends on the side away from you, take the one farthest behind and bring it up and over and then back through the next available space — which will be two spaces over since there are two other weavers.

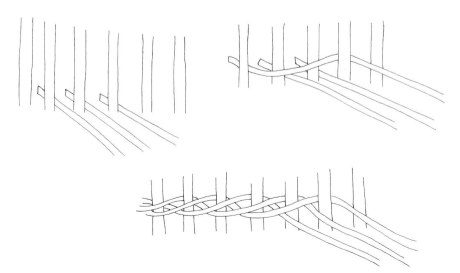

Three rod wale may be done as four rod wale by using four weavers, each going over three and under one. Three and four rod wale are often used at the upsett. Patterns possible with colors and three rod wale:

a) three colors: A number of stakes divisible by three yields vertical stripes.
b) one color plus two natural: A number of stakes divisible by three with a remainder of one yields a variegated outside and a spiral inside.
c) one color plus two natural: A number of stakes divisible by three with a remainder of two yields a spiral outside and a variegated inside.

*Arrow Weave:* The twist of twining or three rod wale may be clockwise or counterclockwise. At any point you may cut off the weavers and insert them to go in the other direction. This will produce an arrow effect in conjunction with the row before.

*Open Weaves:* To make open spaces in the basket, weave in a piece of cardboard the width desired and then weave above it, removing the cardboard when the weaving is secure. It is also possible to make designs with the stakes in open spaces by crossing them as you weave the next row.

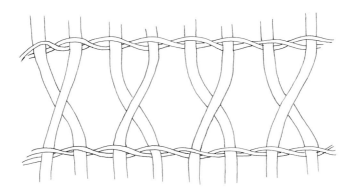

# 7
# Centers

The center I have chosen for the first basket can be made with most any material and can be varied by using colored weavers. I have done it with a piece of colored raffia or yarn. There are many other centers. Here are a few.

One of my students brought me a basket she had made between her first and second classes. The center is a Josephine Knot. She had done it with three strands of #2 rattan using #1 as weavers.

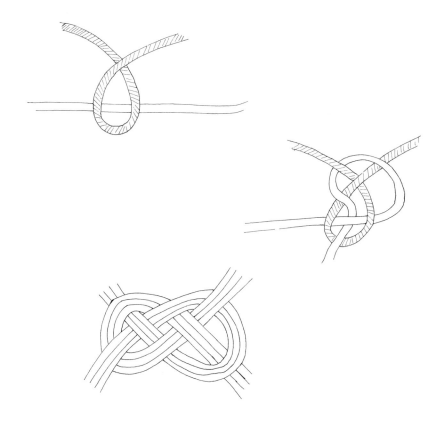

Many students want to learn the center pictured in photos on pages 115, 124, 126, and 127. It is done with twining. Begin with half the stakes and very fine weavers, and weave them together until you have a square in the middle. Do the same thing to the other half. Then lay one square on top of the other so that all four weaver ends are in the same corner. Now you can

a)  begin twining with the two pairs of weavers,
b)  tuck in two of the ends and begin twining with the other two, or
c)  tuck in all four ends and start twining with a new weaver (Fig. 1A).

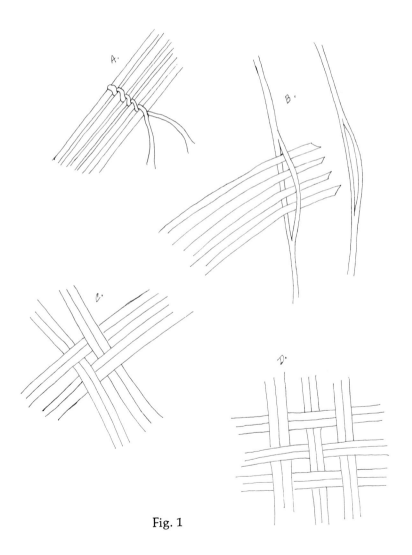

Fig. 1

This is the center of the Indians' watertight baskets. You can make the entire basket in this same weave. By adding stakes you can keep the weave as fine throughout.

*Split Center:* This is a good center for a basket with a flat bottom and for large baskets made of size #5 reed and up, or the equivalent. You can use it with any size reed, though; it is a great way to hide the end of a bye stake.* Any weave may be begun right away but do not break down until the center is big enough for the weave to fit neatly.

Make a split with a sharp knife, mat knife, or awl, in the centers of half of the stakes. Then slip the other half of the stakes through the splits (Fig. 1B).

Figures 1C and 1D and Figure 2A show some other center arrangements.

* See Weaves—In and Out.

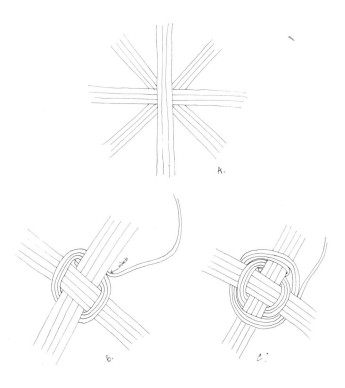

Fig. 2

Figures 2B and 2C show another center technique you may want to use. It is especially good for baskets that will be woven with a single weaver, as well as for its aesthetic values. Begin by tucking the end of the weaver under any group of stakes. Go over and under each group alternately for four rounds. Then pinch the well-soaked weaver and fold it back over the last group and go four more times in the other direction. You can do two rounds each way, and then two each way again, or in any design you like.

*Oval Centers:* Stakes for oval baskets are cut in two lengths. The long stakes should measure the length of the base plus the two end sides plus two border lengths. The short stakes should equal the width of the base plus the sides and borders.

Oval centers tend to "rack" or twist if they are done by the twining weave. To avoid that do only randing (see chapter 6) until the upsett or after (Figs. 3 and 4).

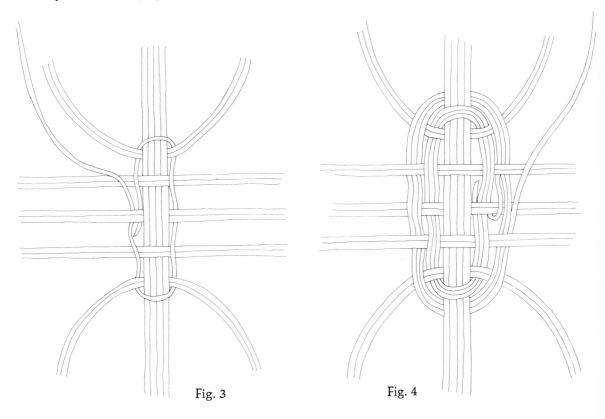

Fig. 3          Fig. 4

*Adding Stakes:* There are two methods I'd like to share. The second I think I invented. (But I also thought I'd invented the use of brambles and then discovered that they have been used honorably for centuries!)

Method 1) This is good for reed- and vine-type baskets. Cut a stake a little bit longer than the length of the stakes in the basket that have not yet been woven upon; the additional length will allow you to insert the new stake into the woven part. Using an awl or similar tool, make a space where the new stake will be added. As you take out the awl, put in the new stake. Then on the next row of weaving, break down to single stakes again. Stakes may be added next to every stake or next to just some, depending on your needs. Stakes can be added later as well.

Method 2) Though these two methods are interchangeable, this one is especially helpful in weaving baskets of grasses, yarns, raffia, or even those materials woven over reed stakes.

Weave until you are ready to add stakes. Cut stakes twice the length of the as-yet-unwoven-upon stakes. Soak the new stakes. Pinch in the center and fold. Hold them in place, or in position, so that your left thumb can hold the point, and simply weave around them as if they were already a part of the basket. It may take a few rounds to get them to stay firm. You have actually added two stakes at a time (Fig. 5).

*Subtracting Stakes:* To make a nice shoulder toward the top edge of a basket, or for any other reason, stakes can be subtracted by weaving two together for a few rows and then either cutting one off or keeping them both as one.

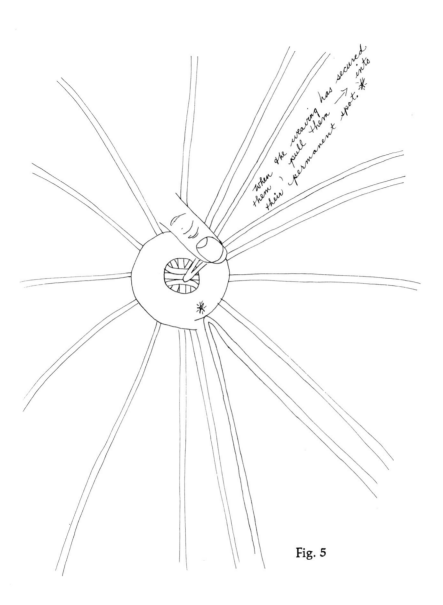

Fig. 5

# 8

# Borders

The basic basket border can be varied by changing the number of stakes that any one stake crosses on either or both rounds. For example, round one might be inside two and out, and round two outside two and back in. My favorite variation is: round one, inside two and out; then round two, outside three or four and back in. The stakes have to be close enough together to keep the border firm.

Another simple closed border is the *Trac* border. This is done in one round. Be sure to leave the first few stakes loose enough to weave the last few back into them. Begin with any stake and weave it in either direction, in-out-in-out, as many times as you choose, or as many times as the shortest standing stake will go.

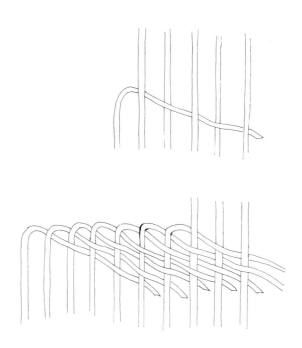

Open borders are not as strong as closed but they are often useful.
Here are a few examples. You can invent your own.

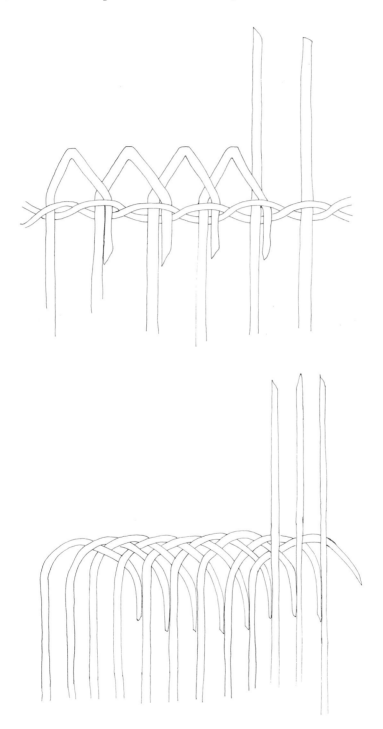

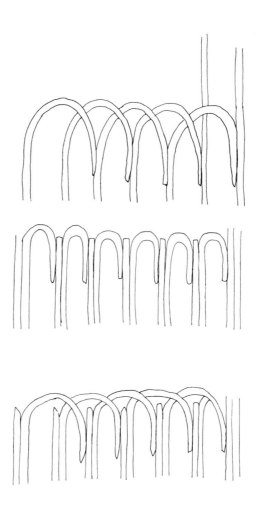

# 9

# Lids

A lid is made just like another basket, turned upside down, then attached if you wish. The difficulty is to make the lid fit the basket. Unless you are making perfectly round baskets, you have to take into account the aberrations of the basket. Try to repeat the spacing of the stakes. By the way, "Never try to make a basket to fit a lid." I read that. Then one day I made a basket that looked like a pretty nice lid, so I tried three times to fit a basket under it before I gave up. I pass on the advice. Weave the lid large enough to cover the border before you upsett, or downsett as it were. Then weave it two or three rows more to accommodate its own border.

If you choose to attach the lid to the basket, you can tie it on with ribbons, yarn, or leather thongs. You can also make hinges out of reed circles with the end wrapped around and around.

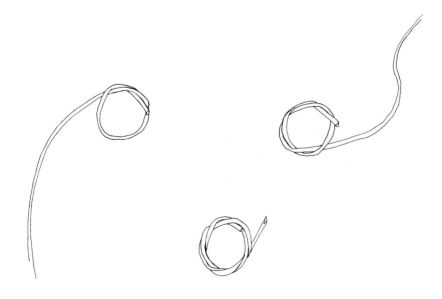

If you want to make a lid that fits just inside the border of the basket, you can make a rim by using any border that leaves the ends of the stakes on the inside of the basket. On these ends work one or two rounds of twining, then the basic border. This sounds complicated but it isn't, though you will want to do your first one, perhaps, on a wide-mouthed basket.

Reed-and-seaweed basket in the doorway.

# 10

# Handles

Handles may be added to a basket for character or design, or they may be made to sling over your arm or grasp in your hand. The first kind you can make any way you want. The second kind must be strong enough to carry the weight of whatever might be put into the basket.

Handles can be made of leather or yarn. Inkle belts or macraméed straps make good handles. They may also be fashioned out of basketry materials. Pottery teapots often have basketry handles because they do not conduct heat.

There are two basic handles I would like to share. Finish the basket first. Handles are made on finished baskets.

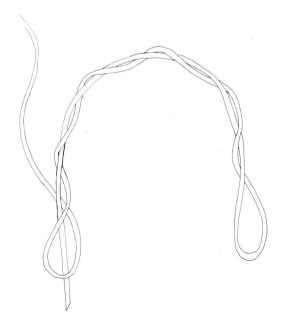

To make the first basic handle, select a long piece of reed, of whatever size you think looks best (usually the same or near the size of the weaver). Soak it. Insert one end under the border. You might hide the end by inserting it down alongside a stake a little way. But have the reed come around to the inside or outside of the border, not up through it. Arch it across the span you have designed and push it under the border on that end. Then bring it back up and wrap it around itself as it goes back across the span again to its beginning. Here the reed must go under the border and back up around itself again to the far side. By then it will have traveled across the span three times. You may finish the handle there by clipping off any excess and hiding the end. Or you can go on back and forth as many times as you wish. You must do at least the first three spans, however, to be sure that the basket is hanging from both sides. You can also add a new piece in the same way if you want a thicker handle or if you want to use two colors. The strength of the handle depends on how many times the reed loops beneath the border.

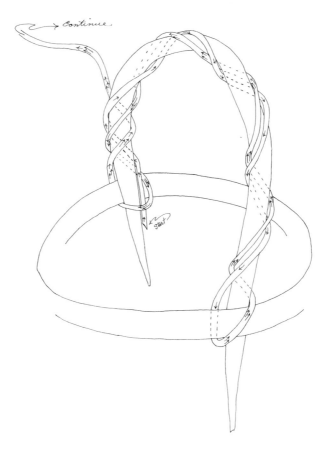

The second style of handle is very similar in construction. It is called a roped handle. Again its strength is dependent on the number of uninterrupted loops of the reed.

You begin with a larger size reed, such as #8, #10, or #12, which is used as the core of the handle. You can also effectively use a green twig or branch or a piece of heavy vine. Before you cut this core piece, hold it up with the basket to design how big an arch you want. Then cut it long enough to make the arch plus enough on each end to go down into the sides of the basket.

With a penknife or a paring knife, shape the ends so that they will fit smoothly down next to a stake. Then insert the core piece. An awl or steel knitting needle may help to make space for it. Next select a long piece of reed of appropriate size. Soak it. Hide the first end next to the core. Then wrap it around the core over to the other side. You don't cover the core this first time. Try three, five, or seven wraps, to find a comfortable slant. An uneven number of twists makes it easier to balance the loops on either side of the basket. I am indebted to one of my students for explaining that to me. On the side opposite the beginning, loop the reed underneath the border and then contrive or design a way to have it go on the same slant as the first crossing. Keep crossing back and forth until you have filled in the core covering. Then hide the end. It may take eight to ten crossings.

# 11

# Lining

*Material needed:* Cardboard, glue, padding for the base, lining material, and thread to match the basket's color.

Cut a cardboard circle to fit inside the base. Cut padding slightly smaller than the cardboard. Cut lining material slightly larger, about an inch all around. Then glue the material around the edge of the cardboard with the padding inside. Cut a strip as long as the circumference of the border plus a half-inch seam allowance at each end and as wide as the height of the sides plus half-inch seam allowances at each edge. Seam the two ends together. Fold under the top edge seam allowance or hem it, and stitch the lining to the inside of the basket just under the border by taking a small stitch in the material and then around a stake. Do not put the needle through the stakes. The stitches won't show because the border helps to hide them. Then run a gathering thread along the bottom edge and gather just enough to fit nicely in the basket. Lay the padded base in and tack it to the bottom edge of the side lining.

# 12

# Colors

There are many good ways to have fun with color in basketry. As I have already suggested, you can weave yarn or twine into reed baskets. Or you can weave baskets solely of yarn or twine. The Aleut Indians use bits of silk threads in their grass baskets. Other possibilities include varnishes, oils, paints, stains, waxes, and dyes. The material can be colored first and then woven or the finished basket may be colored.

*Polishes:* (for reed) I don't think these are good for baskets used with food, but they are excellent for outdoor baskets.

1. Turpentine and varnish, half and half
2. Linseed oil, three parts, and turpentine, one part
3. Stain, one part; turpentine, two parts; and linseed oil, one part
4. Any commercial stain-wax product, thinned with turpentine
5. Any commercial floor wax or furniture polish

*Paints:* Water colors, acrylics or oil paints can be rubbed in or painted on.

*Dyes:* Basket materials can be dyed successfully, and this offers a lot of fun with color and design.

There is a story of an Indian maiden whose betrothed died the night before their wedding day. She spent the next year, aside from her normal tribal duties, making mysterious trips into the mountains. Each time she would return with a small bundle of twigs or a basket of berries or leaves. She also spent many hours in solitary labors. Eventually, it became apparent that she had dyed materials and was subsequently weaving a basket. Then one day, more than a year after her loved one's death, she ceased her solitary activities and once again began to socialize with her peers. When she was asked about the basket, she replied, "On grave." A trip to the burial grounds revealed her year of labor. She had waited for the right seasons not only to gather her basket material but also her colors. The basket was a tribute to her love and a solemn, silent, patient expression of her grief.

I'm not so particular about my colors. I aim to use only native natural dye sources, and whenever I dye anything else, such as curtains, I generally stick some reed in the dye pot too.

There is nothing difficult about dyeing baskets. Because of the nature of the material and the nature of baskets, I feel that colors are more beautiful when they are subtle and do not obscure the natural differences of color in the material. For that reason I recommend, when using packaged analine dyes, that the material be dipped or allowed to rest in the dye bath only one or two minutes at a time. In this way you can see the color density as the material takes color and stop dipping when it is dark enough. Before dyeing reed, wash it first in mild soap and water. Before dyeing raffia, soak it for an hour in cold water. Follow the directions on the package for hand dyeing and remember that color is always darker when it is wet. This is especially true with vines. Also, I was interested to discover that these colors fade and change just as much as natural dyes. I once had a lovely steel gray basket turn brown in a matter of weeks.

Most basket materials are vegetable fibers, which for some reason do not take vegetable colors as readily as do wool or silk. If you are using vegetable dyes, the basket material may be simmered for hours to get the color desired or it may be set on the heater or furnace for a day or two.

I cannot, here, give a complete lesson in natural dyeing, though it is a fascinating activity. I will assume that you can find some of the new books on the subject. What I will do here as I have throughout this book is share an account from my experience. I'll give you my recipe, but I won't guarantee any specific color. I am continually being surprised.

A few years ago I had the opportunity to take part in a dye workshop. Our purpose was to try out as many sources as we could find. Everyone else in the workshop was primarily interested in dyeing wool for weaving. I was forever sticking in little bits of reed. Among the rainbow of colored wools I now have neatly entered into a scrap-book are my drab bits of reed. Their palette runs from tan to drab to murky yellowish, pinkish gray. One of my best colors has been described as "Old Lady Mauve."

Still, it's a lot of fun to say, "Now this one is dyed with onion skins and this color comes from wild grapes." And I am especially attracted to soft dull colors when used in baskets. They seem to give an appearance of age.

To dye reed or raffia in vegetable dyes, you first must "mordant" the material by using a "mordant." The verb means the process of treating the material in a bath of water containing the noun, a metallic salt. The mordant is necessary to hold the color. "Mordant" comes from a Latin word that means "to bite" and apparently that's what it does. Somehow the mordant chains the color to the molecules of the material.

I have heard of dyes that don't need mordants, but as far as I know even the ones that supposedly don't give more color on mordanted material.

The mordants I use are alum, or aluminum potassium sulfate, and tannic acid. (See sources list at end of chapter.) Before mordanting reed, wash it in gentle soap and water, and rinse. Before mordanting raffia, soak it for one hour in cold water.

Here is a cotton mordant recipe. The entire process takes four days. It is good for reed, raffia, peeled honeysuckle, grasses, corn husks, and cattail leaves.

For one pound (dry weight) of material to be dyed, you need the following:

—eight ounces of alum (aluminum potassium sulfate)
— two ounces of washing soda (from the supermarket)
— one ounce of tannic acid (from the drugstore or chemical supply house)

1. Dissolve four ounces of alum and one ounce of washing soda in four to four and a half gallons of cold water; wet your material; immerse it in the bath; heat the mixture slowly and then boil it for one hour; let it cool and leave it in the bath overnight.

2. On the second day, squeeze the material and rinse it in clear soft water; then put it in a bath of one ounce tannic acid and four

to four and a half gallons of soft water; heat the bath to steaming, but not to boiling, and let the material steam for one hour; cool and leave to soak overnight.

3. Repeat the squeezing and rinsing process. Immerse the material in four ounces alum, one ounce washing soda, and four to four and a half gallons water; boil one hour; cool and soak overnight.

4. Squeeze and rinse the material before dyeing. The material may be dried and dyed at a later time.

*Dye Sources:* Raspberry vines and leaves, blackberry vines and leaves, honeysuckle vines and leaves, goldenrod blossoms, marigold blossoms, zinnia blossoms, dahlia blossoms, onion skins (white and red), blackberries, elderberries, pokeberries, sumac berries, viburnum berries, apple twigs and leaves, sassafras tea, dandelion stems and roots, black walnut hulls, wild Concord grapes, Welch's grape juice, fresh coffee grounds, green pine needles, and peanut shells.

You will need about a pound of source material. I use a quart or two of berries and grapes, and a shopping bag half full to full of onion skins, blossoms, twigs, or leaves. The more you use the more color you'll get.

To extract the dye from the source, crush or chop the source substance and cover it with water; soak it overnight; bring it to a boil and simmer it for one hour; strain it through cheesecloth. That's your dye bath.

By the way, black walnut hulls are the one sure color source I know of that doesn't need a mordant. Be sure to wear rubber gloves to handle the hulls or your hands will be dyed, too.

To do the actual dyeing, put the material to be dyed into the dye bath. Heat it to the boiling point but do not boil it. Simmer it for one to two hours. Then take it out of the dye bath and rinse it well.

## SOURCES OF DYE CHEMICALS AND NATURAL DYES

Wide World of Herbs Ltd., 11 Catherine St. East, Montreal, 129 P. Quebec, Canada.
Kem Chemical Co., 545 S. Fulton St., Mt. Vernon, New York 10550.
Straw Into Gold, 5500 College Ave., Oakland, California 94618.
Cushings Perfection Dyes, W. Cushing and Co., Dover-Foxcroft, Maine 04426.

# Gallery of Baskets

This is one of my earliest baskets. I dyed it a soft brown color. It is made all of #4 reed and you can see that I got confused on the border. I was making up a "new" border but I got lost. I like the basket, though, and use it often.

This is a basic basket of unpeeled honeysuckle vine.

Two miniature baskets of copper wire; these are both nearly two inches wide.

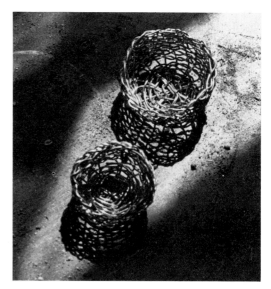

Since I live by the sea, I like to use seaweed in baskets. This basket was made of #5 stakes and #1 and #4 weavers.

This basket is made of #4 reed and brambles and measures approximately eleven inches in diameter.

This is an example of a roped handle, which is explained in chapter 10.

This lady was meant to be a wine bottle cover, but we never have a bottle of wine that lasts long enough to need a cover. She is made in all sorts of improbable basket colors, such as purple.

This was a lot of fun to make. It has no bottom, can stand on either end or lie on its side, and was made to hold kindling or magazines. It stands about 3 feet high, I used the "packing" technique to make its cock-eyed shape and wove in lots of seaweed.

This basket has a grapevine handle and is
made with #5 stakes, #2 and #5 weaver.

This is an example of three rod wale.

I use this "basket" as a soap dish. It has an oval center and a scalloped border.

This center is a combination of Figs. 1C and 2B and 2C.

This is a basic basket of rug yarn. It is white, brown, and black and measures about eight inches across.

This basket is a plain in and out weave of Hong Kong Grass on #6 stakes which I made to hold blocks. It measures about 20 inches high and 22 inches in diameter. Actually I should have made it stronger by using half again as many stakes.

My son, Donick, inside a basket made of #6 and #8 reed.

I had a big harvest of gourds this year, which when harvested but not yet hung to dry seemed to be standing around chatting, or, as they say on Nantucket, "having a gam." They inspired these baskets, which have removable lids. I made them for a friend who is a silversmith to put his wax forms in. I am going to try weaving something around the gourds one of these days.

This is Sue Claflan with her first basket. It is more or less the basic basket but she just made it up as she went along. It is not only beautiful and amazing, it is strong and will work. She made it out of honeysuckle. That night I dreamed I was weaving a basket that was so big I had to stand on the rows of weaving inside of it to continue weaving.

This basket has three rod wale on the lower part of the sides, then twining. The handle is a "roped" ring.

This is an example of three rod wale, which is one of my favorite weaves.

This is raffia woven over #4 reed stakes. The diamonds were inserted by "packing" with the color and then I pushed the rows of weaving down snugly around them.

A student of mine, Maggy Mills, made these and hung them together to hold silverware.

This basket is about five and a half inches across, made of #2 reed woven over two stakes as one.

This is a basic basket by Susan Torgenson,
with a lid that fits inside and rests on a little
rim. It's made of dyed reed and Hong Kong
Grass.

These are of raffia woven over reed stakes.
The largest is about six inches across.

These are some more baskets made of
raffia woven over reed. Notice where the
stakes have been added. None were added
on the smaller basket. They were therefore
so irregularly spaced that I could not make
a border. I wrapped the ends with more
raffia.